in
the
news™

HUNGER

FOOD INSECURITY IN AMERICA

Michael R. Wilson

ROSEN
PUBLISHING®
New York

Published in 2010 by The Rosen Publishing Group, Inc.
29 East 21st Street, New York, NY 10010

Library of Congress Cataloging-in-Publication Data

Wilson, Michael R.
Hunger: food insecurity in America / Michael R. Wilson. — 1st ed.
   p. cm. — (In the news)
Includes bibliographical references and index.
ISBN-13: 978-1-4358-5278-5 (library binding)
ISBN-13: 978-1-4358-5562-5 (pbk)
ISBN-13: 978-1-4358-5563-2 (6 pack)
1. Food supply — United States — Juvenile literature. 2. Hunger — United States — Juvenile literature. I. Title. II. Series.
HD9005.W556 2010
363.8'20973 — dc22

2008047714

Manufactured in the United States of America

On the cover: Clockwise, from upper left: Volunteers prepare meals at a soup kitchen in New York City; a homeless person looks for food in a trash receptacle; lightly stocked shelves at a food pantry in Washington, D.C.

contents

Living on the Edge

1

When it comes to its food supply, the United States of America—the richest country in the world—has always been considered lucky. Known as the "Land of Plenty," it is a place where all people can succeed if they're motivated and if they try hard enough. It's a place where all people can put food on the table, as long as they're willing to work.

Food is grown all over this fertile country. In Florida, fruit literally falls from the trees. In California, thousands of farms produce everything from avocados to zucchini, lettuce by the truckload, and untold bushels and barrels and bags of tomatoes and cucumbers. In the heartland—places like Iowa and Nebraska and Indiana—grains are grown on endless fields, and millions of acres of corn and soybeans get their start. In the high plains of the West, cattle and sheep graze and grow fat. And in all the places in between, on the coasts, and along the borders, there is no shortage of food in the United States. Go to many town squares on a clear Saturday morning, and you will see the local farmer's markets. They bustle with vendors and hungry shoppers happy to be filling their baskets with food. Go to your local supermarket, and you will see the aisles stuffed with frozen dinners, fresh fruits and vegetables, cheese, bread, fish, and meat. There's no doubt about it: This country is full of food. It's everywhere.

America has a seemingly endless supply of crops, like these oranges from Florida.

The Other Side of the Story

It's no surprise, then, that most people in the United States get plenty to eat—three meals a day, at least. And between meals, they snack to their heart's content. They consume what they like, when they like. They may not eat the most nutritious food. They may be prone to eating "junk." But by any measure, they're well fed.

Some Americans, however, are not well fed. Some people in the "Land of Plenty" struggle just to put food on the table. They have no idea where their next meal

Restaurant servers and other low-wage workers are particularly vulnerable to food price increases.

might come from, or how they're going to pay for it. Some just can't afford the food they need. In many cases, these people are hungry.

Who are these people? Often, they're the homeless that you see on the streets in large urban areas. Sometimes, they're the rural working poor—people who have jobs that they go to every day but who, for whatever reason, do not make enough money to pay their bills. Sometimes, they're the elderly—men and women who are living on Social Security checks from the government. They're finding that these checks just are not big enough to cover the costs of housing, medications, and food. Many of those who are hungry have mental or physical disabilities that prevent them from holding down a decent job. Still others have families that are so large, it can be hard to ensure that everyone gets enough to eat.

Food Insecurity: Official Definitions and Statistics

To get a clear picture of food insecurity in the United States, it helps to look at the numbers. The U.S. Department of Agriculture (USDA) defines people who are "food secure" to have access, at all times, to enough food to fuel an active, healthy life for all members of a household. People who are "food insecure," on the other hand, may eat food that is of poor quality, and they may even reduce their food intake. As of 2007, those who were food insecure numbered more than thirty-five million people, more than twelve million of whom were children. Below are the official USDA labels describing the ranges of food security:

High Food Security No reported indications of food-access problems or limitations.

Marginal Food Security One or two reported indications of food-access problems or limitations. Typically, these indications involve worry over a shortage

An empty refrigerator can be a stark reminder of just how painful it is to go without food.

of food in the household, but with little or no indication of changes in diets or food intake.

Low Food Security Reports of reduced quality, variety, or desirability of diet. Little or no indication of reduced food intake.

Very Low Food Security Reports of multiple indications of disrupted eating patterns and reduced food intake.

In its efforts to understand food insecurity in the United States, the USDA has compiled numerous research reports based on surveys of U.S. households. Although only a small percentage of households are by definition "food insecure," the reports make it clear that food insecurity is a serious issue.

Based on data from the USDA Economic Research Service's December 2007 Current Population Survey Food Security Supplement:

- 89 percent of U.S. households (103 million) are "food secure" year-round
- 11 percent of U.S. households (12.6 million) experience food insecurity. This means that, for whatever reason, there is not enough food for all members of the family
- About a third of food-insecure households (4 percent of all U.S. households, or 4.6 million households) experience "very low food security." This means that household members have to eat less food than they normally would because they cannot afford to eat their normal diet
- Almost 7 percent of U.S. households (8 million) have "low food security"
- About two-thirds of "food insecure" households are forced to eat simpler diets, take part in federal food and nutrition assistance programs, obtain emergency food from community resources like food pantries and kitchens, or take other measures to avoid serious disruptions to their food consumption
- A typical "food secure" household spends at least 30 percent more on food than a typical "food insecure" household of the same size

The USDA's 2007 data digs even deeper into the issue of U.S. food security. For example, the USDA uses its surveys to determine how frequently and for how long those households that experienced food insecurity were actually food insecure. Here, again, are the findings:

- About a third of the households that experience "very low food security" do so occasionally— that is, for one or two months of the year
- About two-thirds of households experience "very low food security" for three or more months of the year
- Around 20 percent of households were deemed "food insecure," and 30 percent of those deemed to have "very low food security" experience food insecurity almost constantly throughout the year
- The average household experiencing food insecurity is food insecure at some time during six months of the year
- The average household experiencing "very low food security" is food insecure at some time during seven months of the year

The Difference Between Food Insecurity and Hunger

Hunger is not the same thing as food insecurity. It is, however, a potential effect of food insecurity that is

Survey Says: Times Are Tough

The USDA 2006 survey took a close look at U.S. households that were determined to have "very low food security." Of those who completed the survey:

- 98 percent said that they were worried their food would run out before they got money to buy more
- 96 percent said that the food they bought did not last and they did not have money to get more
- 94 percent said that they could not afford to eat balanced meals
- 95 percent said that an adult in the household had cut the size of meals or skipped meals because there was not enough money for food
- 95 percent said that they had eaten less than they would have because there was not enough money for food
- 69 percent said that they had been hungry but did not eat because they could not afford food
- 46 percent said that they lost weight because they did not have enough money for food
- 33 percent said that an adult in the household did not eat for a whole day because there was not enough money for food

Conditions in households with children were similar, but the reported food-insecure conditions of both adults and children were taken into account.

In many urban areas in particular, it's not uncommon for volunteers to hand out food to those in need.

very serious. For the USDA, hunger, by definition, is a "weakened condition brought about by prolonged lack of food." When people experience food insecurity, they may lack food altogether or they may have some food, but it's not enough. On the other hand, they may have plenty of food to survive and to avoid hunger, but it's not the food that they would choose to eat given different circumstances. Many people, for example, will go to so-called food banks to get a meal when they can't afford to put one together themselves. These people are, by definition, "food insecure." But because they are able to obtain food and are not necessarily malnourished, they are not classified as "hungry."

Hunger is one potential consequence of food insecurity, but it's not the only one. People who are food insecure may also experience severe stress or anxiety, for example. Imagine what it must feel like for adults who are unable to afford groceries for the children who are relying on them. They might feel embarrassed or ashamed. They might become depressed. Their children might not starve and, ultimately, might never miss a meal. But being food insecure is a state of being that no individual wants to be in. This is especially true for a mother or a father.

Up and Up . . . and Up: The Cost of Food

How do individuals who can barely pay their rent, put gas in their car, or buy clothes and shoes afford to put enough food on the table so their families can eat? It's an unfortunate dilemma faced by millions in the United States. The price of almost everything is going up, and many people aren't making enough money to keep pace. As they have watched their rent payments double, they have lost the very homes where they have lived and raised families. As they have paid more and more for health care, they have been left with less to spend on other necessities. When they have watched the price of gas go through the roof, climbing upwards of $3 and $4 per gallon, they have reduced the amount of driving they did, or they simply have gotten rid of their cars altogether. Living in the twenty-first century has been anything but cheap. And for those who have less—the poor and struggling— it hurts even more.

The Price of Food

If you've paid attention in the grocery store, then you've seen it yourself: Prices are skyrocketing on everything from cheese, eggs, meat, and bread to cereals and canned goods. Almost every day there are stories in the news about mothers with small children who can't believe what they're paying for milk. Or, even worse, mothers with infants who have to water down their baby formula to make it go further and fill up their babies' bellies, even if it means that their babies won't get the nutrients they need to thrive. It's a tough spot for many people. They simply cannot afford the food they need.

The price that consumers pay for food depends on many different factors. In a free market economy, there's supply and demand. This theory of market value says that when more people want something, those who are selling it can get more money for it. That's good for the sellers but not so good for the buyers. As our country's population—and the world's population—grows and there are more mouths to feed, food production must keep pace. If it doesn't, then that means there is less food to go around, which drives up the cost.

Consider this one example of increased demand, from just across the U.S. border in Mexico. That country imports much of its wheat from the United States, and

Consumer prices in the United States are rising faster than they have in many years.

its appetite for wheat-based products is growing. Since more Mexican companies are competing to buy U.S. wheat, the price of U.S. wheat—and the price of food made with it—is going up.

A Global Market

Mexico is not the only country importing food from the United States and, thereby, increasing demand for the

food grown on U.S. soil. The
market for food is a global
one. All you have to do is
look at the booming populations in China, India, and
elsewhere. With billions of
people walking the planet,
and many of them growing
wealthier by the day, the
demand for food becomes
almost overwhelming. In
addition, many of these
individuals want higher-

A supermarket in Beijing, China,
carries a selection of American
breakfast cereals.

quality, more expensive food. They're more than willing
to pay extra to have it shipped from across the world—
from places like the United States. In other words, it's not
only supply and demand. It's global supply and demand.

Biofuels: Increasing the Burden

Another factor contributing to the price of food, and
also related to supply and demand, is U.S. government–
mandated biofuel production. Laws now require that
large portions of certain crops, such as corn, go toward
the production of fuels like ethanol. These fuels, called
biofuels, are derived from vegetable materials. They can
be added to gasoline to make it burn cleaner. Burning
biofuels is better for the environment than burning

conventional fuels, but producing biofuels has affected food production. Farmers are now under pressure to sell their crops not only to the companies that want to process them for food but also to companies that want to turn them into fuel. It's up for debate just how big a role biofuel production is playing in the rising cost of food, but it's widely agreed that such production is at least one of the factors.

Growing corn for fuel affects the price in other ways, too. For example, land formerly used to grow a variety of crops is now dedicated only to corn. Much of the U.S. food supply depends on corn for feed. This is the case with factory-farmed cows and pigs especially. In addition, the most common sweetener in processed food is high-fructose corn syrup, which is made from corn. With less corn available, hog farms and processed food makers must pay more to produce their food items. The increase in the cost of production is inevitably passed on to the consumer in higher prices.

Oil

Dig a little deeper and the supply-and-demand problem widens. Oil is also used to heat our homes and offices, fuel our airplanes, and power the engines and generators that keep America humming. Food production is highly reliant on oil. Oil fuels the tractors that harvest our crops. It puts gas and diesel in the trucks, trains, and

Large American companies transport their food products all over the country—and the world. When fuel costs rise, the additional expense is passed on to the consumer in higher prices.

boats that ship our food from state to state and around the world. As it currently stands, without oil, our food supply would be crippled. The price of food, then, depends in large part on the price of oil. As the price of oil goes up, so, too, does the price of food. The price of oil fluctuates every single day, but it depends in large part on forces far removed from the lives of grocery store shoppers. Or, so it may seem.

One factor influencing the price of oil is unrest in the Middle East, where much of the world's oil is produced.

Among the reasons for the unrest are the U.S. occupation of Iraq and the fears of nuclear ambition in neighboring Iran. These two countries have large oil reserves. With the constant back-and-forth wrangling between the powers that hold the oil "over there" and the powers that want the oil "over here," it's anyone's guess what one barrel of oil will cost at the end of any given day.

Thanks to their obsession with driving, Americans consume more oil (in the form of gasoline) than anyone else in the world. To bring down the cost of food, one obvious solution would be to do less driving. With fewer cars on the road, demand for oil would decrease. That, in turn, would drive its price down. Unfortunately, this is not a likely solution, as few Americans are willing to give up their cars.

In recent years, there has been heightened interest in the use of renewable power sources that don't rely on oil. These include solar electricity, nuclear power, geothermal energy, and hybrid electric cars. It remains to be seen if renewable sources of energy will one day make oil obsolete. If they do, then transportation will be cheaper and you can be sure the price of food will fall.

Water

The cost of securing water is another factor in the price of food. America's huge farms require huge amounts of water to irrigate fields and water livestock. The problem is, there is often not enough water to go around. And when those farms are located in drought-prone areas like California and the Southwest, maintaining the water supply can be even more expensive.

Farms require enormous amounts of water—and farmers often pay a hefty price to keep that water flowing.

Where water is scarce, it must be shipped in with big tanker trucks (using expensive diesel fuel) or diverted across entire states along pipelines. The increased cost of delivering the water is directly reflected in the price of food.

No End in Sight

Recent years have seen the price of big commodity foods like corn, wheat, and soybeans rise faster than they have in a long time. In 2007 alone, food prices rose by 4 percent—the greatest percentage gain since the early 1990s. While consumers here in the United States are feeling the burden of these price hikes, they're not alone. There have been food-related riots in Mexico; demonstrations in Italy; and protests in India, Indonesia, and Africa. Some are saying that the fight to secure affordable food will be the biggest challenge of the twenty-first century. Will the price of food continue to rise? If you are going with most experts on the subject, then you wouldn't bet against it.

How People Cope

It hurts when an individual first realizes that he or she can't afford to eat. And it is especially difficult when there are other mouths to feed—children, a spouse, elderly parents, or grandparents. The despair of knowing that there isn't enough money to buy life's most important necessity can be utterly overwhelming.

When it comes down to it, there really is no more important expense than food. We must eat and drink to survive. It's that simple. So, as grocery stores continue to stock their shelves but prices go up and up, what are those on the edge—the poor, the "food insecure," the hungry—doing to get by?

One obvious solution arrived at by some is to eat less. As mentioned above, news reports tell of mothers who water down their infant formulas to make it go further, knowingly or unknowingly putting their babies' lives in danger. Others who are struggling may put less food on the table at each meal, getting by with smaller portions, without "seconds" or desserts. Many parents will cut back on their personal food consumption while continuing to feed their children as much as they need. It's not uncommon for people to skip meals altogether—foregoing breakfast or lunch, or both, and saving their money for dinner.

Another solution has been to eat foods that are cheaper. Take a stroll through the grocery store and you'll see that there are major differences in food prices from one aisle to the next. Highly processed foods and so-called junk foods almost always cost less and pack more calories than less processed food items. Many people will choose these cheaper foods every time, motivated by their price rather than their nutritional value. Unfortunately, nutritional quality tends to decline with the price. Those calories are often "empty." In other words, they are mainly provided by cheap sugar. So, as people eat poor-quality food to save money, they're also robbing themselves of a healthy diet.

Then, there are the not-so-obvious solutions to obtaining food on the cheap. For example, some resort to urban foraging, or "Dumpster diving," which means scrounging edible food out of waste receptacles at grocery stores and restaurants. Dumpster diving allows people to get high-quality food at no cost. The food may have expired use-by dates, or be packaged in dented or torn containers, or have minor blemishes. Imagine all the food that is not finished and then thrown out at a restaurant, or simply tossed into the garbage at schools,

The U.S. Department of Agriculture has estimated that Americans waste fifty million tons of perfectly edible food annually.

sporting events, and even in residential neighborhoods, and you can see what Dumpster divers are on to. Yes, Dumpster diving may be desperate and a bit demeaning, but when people are hungry, they will do almost anything in order to eat.

Desperation leads to yet another solution to finding food: crime. In some cases, people will steal to get the food that they need to survive. They will break into houses, mug people on the street, steal cash out of cars, or rob convenience stores. Shoplifting inevitably goes up with the price of food, as desperate individuals steal what they cannot afford in order to stave off hunger.

Food Assistance Programs

One way that food-insecure households stave off hunger is through participation in one of the three major federal food and nutrition assistance programs. These programs are the Food Stamp Program, the National School Lunch Program, and the Special Supplemental Nutrition Program for Women, Infants, and Children (WIC). Others obtain supplemental food from emergency food providers in their community or through one of the twelve other federal programs administered by the USDA's Food and Nutrition Service.

The Food Stamp Program (FSP) provides monthly benefits for low-income households to purchase food items at grocery stores. Recent figures from the USDA show that nearly twenty-seven million Americans par-ticipate in the program, receiving, on average, about $94 per person per month.

The National School Lunch Program operates in nearly 100,000 schools throughout the country. The program provides free or reduced-price lunches to students from low-income families. Every school day, around thirty million children participate in the program.

A Helping Hand

Many families could not afford to eat without the help of food assistance programs like those offered by the federal government and local communities. Some statistics and figures on the use of such programs in 2006, the most recent year with information available, are:

- 3.8 million U.S. households (3.3 percent of all households) accessed emergency food from a food pantry at least once
- 56 percent of food-insecure households participated in one of the three major federal food assistance programs
- 65 percent of food pantries, 61 percent of emergency kitchens, and 52 percent of emergency shelters reported an increase in the number of people using their food services
- Feeding America provided emergency food assistance to an estimated twenty-five million low-income people

The WIC program provides grants to states, which then distribute the money in the form of vouchers. Low-income families with children under the age of five can use the vouchers to purchase food, as can low-income women who are pregnant or just had a baby. In 2006, the average monthly benefit for individuals who use WIC was about $37.

Finally, local food pantries and emergency kitchens are the primary sources of emergency food assistance. There are thousands of food pantries and emergency kitchens throughout the country. They provide millions of meals to individuals and families who otherwise might go hungry. Food pantries and emergency kitchens are typically run by volunteers and are supported by donations from the community.

The USDA reports that slightly more than half of all food-insecure households participated in at least one of the three major federal food and nutrition assistance programs. In addition, around half of such households obtained emergency food from a food pantry at some time during the year.

For many in the United States, food stamps, linked to debit cards like this one, are a way of life.

Demographics of
Food Insecurity:
The People

If you have never gone without a meal, then you are lucky. You have never experienced hunger. You don't know what it's like to eat less food, or poor-quality food, because your family was unable to afford the food that they needed. So, who are the people who are food insecure? Who is going hungry, and where are they?

The prevalence of food insecurity varies by household type. According to USDA data from 2007, nationwide, 11 percent of households experience food insecurity. Certain households are more likely than others to be food insecure. For example, households with incomes below the official poverty line make up more than 36 percent of the food insecure. (The official poverty line varies from year to year.) Households with children are almost twice as likely as those without children to experience food insecurity. Households with children that are headed by a single woman make up more than 30 percent of the food insecure. Families where the parents are married are less likely to be food insecure.

Black households make up almost 22 percent of the food insecure, while Hispanic households make up almost 20 percent. White, non-Hispanic households make up about 8 percent of the food insecure.

The prevalence of food insecurity also depends on where households are located. Households in the southern United States, for example, are more likely than those elsewhere in the nation to be food insecure. Households in the Northeast are less likely than others to be food insecure. Households in big cities are more likely to experience food insecurity than those in suburban areas. Households in rural areas are less likely than households in urban areas to experience food insecurity, yet rates of food insecurity in rural areas are slightly higher than the national average. It is a sad twist that many of the households with low food security are in the very farm communities that produce low-cost, wholesome food for the rest of America and the world.

Certain segments of the population are more likely to experience "very low food security" than the national average of 4 percent of households. For example, the USDA's 2007 data shows that 10 percent of families with children headed by single women are in this category. Eight percent of black households and 5.7 percent of Hispanic households are in this category. So, too, are 15 percent of the households living below the federal poverty line and 5 percent of the households in major

Family meals at the dinner table may become trying when there's not enough food to go around.

cities. Slightly more than 4 percent of southern households experienced "very low food security."

The USDA has compiled some interesting statistics regarding the 4 percent of households in the United States that are considered to have "very low food security." Such households include:

- 2.1 percent of all married couples with children
- 2.6 percent of all multiple-adult households with no children
- 1.8 percent of all households with elderly people

Food Insecurity by State

Food security is definitely a national issue. To learn more about it, the USDA studied several years of data (2004–2006) to determine how the populations in individual states were experiencing food insecurity relative to those in others. In general, states in the Midwest and the Northeast had lower rates of food insecurity than elsewhere. States in the South had higher rates than elsewhere. Taking all states into consideration, the prevalence of "food insecurity" ranged from 6.4 percent in North Dakota to 18.1 percent in Mississippi. The prevalence of "very low food security" ranged from 2.1 percent in New Jersey to 6.4 percent in Mississippi. For obvious reasons, states that tend to be home to individuals and families with higher incomes experience lower rates of food insecurity than those with people who, on average, earn less.

Poverty: Living Below the Line

It should come as no surprise that there is a very close correlation between poverty, food insecurity, and hunger. After all, it's the poor who cannot afford to buy food. It's the poor who often must choose between paying the bills that keep their household running and paying for the meals that keep everyone well fed.

Top Ten Food-Insecure States

According to USDA data compiled between 2004 and 2006, 11.3 percent of U.S. households are reportedly food insecure. The ten states listed below have the highest prevalence of food-insecure households:

- Mississippi: 18.1 percent
- New Mexico: 16.1 percent
- Texas: 15.9 percent
- South Carolina: 14.7 percent
- Oklahoma: 14.6 percent
- Utah: 14.5 percent
- Louisiana: 14.4 percent
- Arkansas: 14.3 percent
- Kentucky: 13.6 percent
- Arizona: 13.1 percent

Tunica County, Mississippi, is one of the poorest counties in the United States. One in three families there lives below the poverty line.

Unfortunately, poverty in the United States is on the rise, according to the nonprofit grassroots advocacy group RESULTS. This organization works to get elected officials to implement laws and policies that reduce hunger and poverty. RESULTS says that there are more Americans living in poverty today than there were in the year 2000. (The 2008 federal poverty guidelines set the poverty line at an income of $22,200 for a family of four.) Overall, between 12 and 13 percent of U.S. households live in poverty. The most recent U.S. Census statistics show that there are around thirty-seven million people living in poverty in the United States.

Meanwhile, as RESULTS points out, more and more Americans are participating in the federal Food Stamp Program. This is a clear sign that U.S. families are having a tough time putting food on the table. "The struggles families are facing across the country to make ends meet are very real," said RESULTS domestic campaign manager Meredith Dodson. "While the price of food goes up, the average food stamp benefit remains at $1 per person per meal."

Many are calling on the U.S. Congress to take measures to ease the pain. Some are requesting that outdated food stamp benefits more accurately reflect the price of a meal in the United States. Others are asking for expansion of the Child Tax Credit (CTC). This is a tax refund that goes out to many families with children.

In 2008, Reno, Nevada, set up a "tent city" for its homeless when existing shelters became overcrowded.

"While expanding the CTC will not solve the larger problem of more Americans living in poverty, it will provide urgently needed relief to struggling families," Dodson said.

The "Invisible" Hungry

In urban areas especially, many of the hungriest people are the homeless, the addicted, and the outcast. They are often referred to as "invisible" because in many cases, they are simply ignored. These are the people you see living in boxes on the street, tucked beneath a blanket in a dark corner of a building, or riding the subway, back and forth, with nowhere else to go. They are the people who beg from you as you walk by, asking for whatever you can spare.

Many cities maintain homeless shelters for these people. Shelters are warm, dry places where the homeless can go to spend the night and eat a meal. Sometimes, however, shelters fill up. Or, there is not

Poverty Statistics

Here are a few facts about the prevalence of poverty in the United States, courtesy of Feeding America, the nation's largest charitable hunger-relief group:

- About 37 million people, or between 12 and 13 percent of the population, live in poverty
- 7.6 million families live in poverty
- 20.2 million people age eighteen to sixty-four live in poverty
- 12.8 million children under the age of eighteen live in poverty
- 3.4 million people age sixty-five and older live in poverty

enough food to go around. Or, the people who could most use the shelters are in such dire straits—for instance, they may be sick, drunk, or high—that they never find their way there.

These "invisible" people are the hungriest of the hungry. They are in such difficult circumstances that they often will forgo food just so they can afford another round of drugs. Or, if not addicted, they are unable to work because of mental or physical disabilities and, therefore, are unable to pay for a decent meal, let alone a place to live.

Hunger and Health Consequences

When people go hungry, they risk serious health problems. We need calories to survive, and we get them from food. Calories give us energy and, thus, are fuel for our bodies—the very thing that makes our hearts tick, our muscles move, and our lungs work.

When people are deprived for a long time of the calories that they need, their malnourished bodies begin to break down.

Poor nutrition caused developmental delays and serious health issues in this young girl, prior to her being adopted.

Their health deteriorates. They become more susceptible to disease and injury. Their muscles become weak. In the most extreme cases, people can die. Starvation, while not common in the United States, is far too common elsewhere in world. One only needs to see the images of starving children in sub-Saharan Africa to understand just how serious hunger can be.

Many of those who battle hunger must also deal with the conditions brought on by their malnourishment. Mental health, for example, begins to deteriorate. An individual may begin to lose a personal sense of purpose or well-being, especially when he or she is unable to provide children with the bare necessities. Depression may set in.

Hunger can rock a person to the core. Compared to everything else in life, there is nothing more important than sustenance—eating enough to survive. When the food one needs just to get up in the morning is not available, this takes a tremendous toll on both the body and the mind.

Food Insecurity and the Most Vulnerable

Almost everyone agrees that the most vulnerable among us deserve special protection and attention. When children, the elderly, the mentally ill, and the physically disabled can't obtain adequate nutrition in order to lead a healthy life, others must stand up for them. In the United States, this sort of care takes place all of the time, thanks to food banks, emergency kitchens, food stamps, local food drives led by Parent-Teacher Associations (PTAs), Boy Scouts, Girl Scouts, and similar efforts. For the most part, these programs work wonders: People who would otherwise go hungry get food to eat.

But why should children ever lack the resources to put food in their mouths? And why should those who physically cannot get work and make a living, and who cannot make the money they need to buy food, go hungry? What does this say about our society and its values?

Children

According to government research, at least twelve million children live in food-insecure households in the United States. An additional three million children live in households that are either hungry or are on the edge of hunger. Households with children report food difficulties at almost double the rate of households that do not have children. Overall, less than 1 percent of all households in the United States report their children have ever gone hungry. However, 81 percent of food-insecure households report feeding their children low-cost, less varied foods in order to save money. And more than 50 percent say their children have eaten meals that weren't balanced because they couldn't afford good food.

In many cases, it's the children who go hungry last, as the adults in a household cut back on their own food intake first. Adults may skip meals and eat less to make sure that their children can fill their plates. Nevertheless, children are deprived of the food that they need in an alarming number of cases.

One way in which adults can obtain food for their hungry children is through school lunch programs. At school, their children are guaranteed access to the food they need throughout the day. Depending on the financial resources of the parent, school meals may be free, or

School lunch programs help children who can't get the nutrition they need at home.

they may be offered at a substantial discount. The U.S. government subsidizes (partially pays for) these programs.

Some questions have been raised about school lunch programs and their effectiveness. On the school lunch line, it's often obvious who is getting a free meal and who is paying full price. This might cause older children to avoid eating subsidized meals because of the stigma (real or perceived dishonor) that's associated with it. Many children don't want their friends to know that their family is poor. So, instead of eating, they'll pretend they are not hungry and skip school meals.

Schools are learning how to address this problem. Some are doing away with the visible vouchers and, instead, are using electronic systems that allow all children to go through the same lines to get their food. By not segregating those who do receive discounted meals from those who don't, it's harder to tell who is paying and who is not. Schools that have tried this approach report that more students are eating subsidized meals.

In the end, ensuring that children have enough to eat is critically important to their health. Without adequate nutrition, everything from brain development to bone and muscle growth is at risk. There are other problems associated with hunger in children as well. For example, research has suggested that children who don't get enough to eat have trouble fitting in among their classmates and have increased difficulty with schoolwork. Children may feel outcast, neglected, ignored, and even ashamed. Being hungry is never good. When children are hungry, it's even worse.

Seniors and Other Dependents

As a group, seniors and other dependents—the mentally and physically disabled—are in many ways like children. Some are dependent on caregivers for all of their basic needs, i.e., food, clothing, and shelter. When those caregivers are struggling themselves, it's not uncommon for their dependents to suffer, too.

America's massive baby boomer generation is now well into their sixties. In the coming decades, more and more seniors are likely to need care. Many of them will rely on federal assistance for their financial well-being,

Meals on Wheels delivers food to those in need. Unfortunately, when food and fuel costs rise, many such hunger-relief programs are put in jeopardy.

while others will rely on family, friends, or professional caregivers. Thanks to improvements in health care, life expectancy in the United States is increasing all the time. This means that people can expect to live much longer than they used to. But it also means that they will need to make their money stretch further to get them through their final years. Those who are well off have less to worry about. But those who are poor (or even worse, poor and in poor health) may get into trouble.

Again, there are safeguards that help prevent hunger among the elderly. For example, Meals on Wheels programs bring food directly to the homes of those who are immobile and can't get out to shop on their own. The government has the taxpayer-funded Social Security program. It provides monthly payments to retirees, which they can use to help pay their bills. Many communities maintain senior centers that provide cheap or free meals. Similar outreach programs, plus federal and state assistance, help the mentally and physically disabled. The disabled also benefit from the good hearts of their friends and neighbors.

Many argue that feeding seniors and other dependents is just as important as feeding our children. It's an easy case to make. After all, why should anyone go hungry in the "Land of Plenty"?

When Disaster Strikes

Not long ago, when Hurricane Katrina hit the Gulf Coast of the United States, thousands of families were displaced from their homes. A few had relatives that they could go to, and others could afford to move to hotels until their homes were repaired. But countless others were suddenly homeless and dependent on whatever shelters were provided by religious organizations and state and federal authorities. Needless to say, many people were also hungry. They lacked kitchens for making their meals, and many were suddenly without the jobs that they depended on for income to buy food. A lot of people suddenly found themselves in serious trouble.

Disasters like Katrina, other hurricanes, tornadoes, and tsunamis are common causes of hunger, even here in the United States. When people lose their homes and their jobs, they often lose the ability to feed their families as well. In most cases, there are adequate community resources to shelter those in need and to provide meals temporarily. Homeless shelters open their doors. Donations of food and money come pouring in to community food banks. As long as the emergency is short-lived, nearly everyone finds a place to sleep and enough to eat.

Unfortunately, though, this isn't always the case, as some communities are less prepared for such disasters than others. Hurricane Katrina made it clear that serious calamities have serious consequences. While some of those consequences are obvious—death and destroyed homes—others, such as hunger, are not.

Solutions and the Future

Each year in the United States, millions of people go hungry. It's a fact. So, what can we do about it? And what is being done right now? To answer this question yourself, just look outside your door. You'll see the world in action. Farmers are working the land to grow bountiful, nutritious crops. Trucks are transporting that food from the farm to the people who will eat it. Community activists are asking their government officials to enact new and better policies that will provide more help for the needy. Everyday people are going to work to earn the money they need to purchase food for their families. And various charitable organizations are doing what they do best, day in and day out: caring for those who can't care for themselves.

You will also see homeless people begging for money and for food. You will see people in long lines at local employment agencies, hoping to land a job, even if it's just for one day. In addition, there are people filling their bowls, and those of their children, at emergency kitchens. And you will see kids on the lunch line who seem just a little skinnier, and hungrier, than those around them.

A Complex Problem

There is no clear solution to hunger and food insecurity. Yet, while hunger is a huge challenge in the United States, it's not an impossible one. One clear path to improving the situation is through changes in public policy—the laws our government puts in place to protect the needy. Some groups are calling for expansion of the federal, state, and local "food safety nets." These are the programs designed to prevent families from falling into positions of food insecurity. Expansion, of course, requires money. So, the bottom line is funding. If voters can convince their representatives to allot more money to public assistance programs, then those programs will better serve all of those in need.

Another part of the solution is education. There is a clear link between poverty and poor education. High school dropouts make far less money than high school graduates. College graduates earn more than those who merely finish high school. The argument, then, is to provide the resources that people need to go to school and get a good education. Through a good education,

This salad bar at an elementary school in Chicago is the result of a new federal law stating that all U.S. schools must establish wellness policies.

they can land good jobs. And with good jobs, they'll never go hungry.

There are other solutions to food insecurity as well. Put an end to discrimination against minorities and women, and they'll have an easier time finding jobs that pay as well as those that are offered to men. Mend the economy, which heavily favors the wealthy, so that there's less of an income gap between the richest among us and the poorest. Help families stay together and, thereby, improve the chances that children in those families will be raised in an environment that is both nurturing and financially secure. Improve treatment programs for those addicted to drugs and those battling mental illness. All of these steps are necessary if hunger is to be abolished in America.

Community Food Security

What is the best way to ensure that people get all the food that they need to lead healthy lives? Many experts on food security claim there is no better way than by relying on local communities to get the job done. In a community, after all, people know the individuals in need. They are the next-door neighbors, or the woman they see walking down the street every afternoon with children in tow. It makes sense that community members would lend a helping hand to those around them who could use it.

With this in mind, the USDA and others have been using the term "community food security." Community food security is centered on prevention. The idea is that no one will go hungry as long as there are community-based resources to turn to when necessary. As the USDA explains, "Community food security focuses on the underlying social, economic, and institutional factors within a community that affect the quantity, quality, and affordability of food." In other words, communities should work to put local resources to good use, including community gardens, farmer's markets, and emergency food assistance programs. Such efforts could help guide individuals out of poverty, freeing them from the accompanying struggle to afford food. Ideally, all people in a community would eventually reach a position of food security, where they never lack the food that they and their families need to be healthy. Community food security addresses everything from food availability and affordability to health problems related to diet to farmland preservation to job opportunities.

So, what are some examples of community food security in action? Outreach programs help identify families that qualify for food stamps and make it easier for them to get food stamps they can use at local grocery stores. Farmer's markets provide good, fresh food that is sometimes more affordable than the food available in supermarkets. Community gardens provide small plots of land where low-income individuals and families can produce at least some of their own food. And food recovery programs take edible food from restaurants and stores that would otherwise be thrown away and give it to groups that can redistribute it to those in need.

Another important part of food security is ensuring that local farmers can make a decent living by selling their products to the community. When farms sell locally, their food can often be sold at lower prices than food shipped across the country or from other parts of the world. The benefits are twofold: First, people in the community have access to more affordable food. And second, farmers stick around and their land remains in agriculture instead of being converted to other uses.

When individuals can grow their own food, it reduces food costs, which in turn helps to alleviate food insecurity.

The Global Food Crisis

While there are people here in the United States who struggle to put food on the table, this country is by no means the only one with hungry citizens. Individuals and families from all over the world face similar hunger problems. In most cases, those problems are far worse.

The world population is now growing faster than it ever has before. Some even say the current rate of growth is not sustainable, that it must slow down—or even reverse—if humanity is to survive. Meanwhile, even as more and more people fill the streets of cities in all regions of the globe, those same people are, overall, growing wealthier. Countries that at one point provided all the food their people needed from within their own borders are now importing food to meet the demands of a larger and wealthier population. Whereas once these people merely needed rice, now, with more money to spend, they want goods like meat.

The huge increase in demand has put more pressure on the world's natural resources. Great swaths of land are being cleared of trees to provide ground for new farms. Huge factory farms are swelling with livestock and polluting the air and water. All the while, a greater amount of oil is being burned to produce and distribute it all. And, at the same time, more people are being left behind. While some grow rich and eat more and better food, others grow poorer and find that they have less and less to eat. As a result, in some places like parts of Africa, societies fall apart. Droughts, wars, and famines set in. Large populations are forced to pick up their possessions and move, putting pressure on neighboring regions to provide food and shelter. People go hungry. Children starve. It's the world at its worst. Something must be done. Whether it takes political arrangements,

These children in Chad, Africa, know the anguish of food insecurity. War caused them to flee their homes and live in refugee camps.

peace agreements, trade pacts, humanitarian aid, or an approach that combines all of these things into one, somehow it must come to an end.

Food and the Future

The picture here in the United States is not nearly as grim as it is in some other parts of the world. Still, for those who are hungry in this country, the situation is serious. The United States prides itself on being a democracy, on being a place where anyone can succeed and all people stand on equal footing. Unfortunately, as long as there are people within its borders who lack the food that they need to survive, that "promise," as it is, seems empty.

Whether that promise rings true in the future is anyone's guess. Chances are, it's up to people like you—today's youth, tomorrow's leaders—to make sure that it does. It won't be easy. It will take work. But that's what the American dream is all about.

Glossary

advocacy The act of supporting a cause that typically has wider social implications.

calamity A disastrous event that often results in a loss of life and/or property.

calorie A unit of food energy.

demeaning Degrading; lowering in value or status.

famine An extreme lack or scarcity of food.

farmer's markets Outdoor markets where local farmers sell their goods to the community.

food bank A place where food is contributed and distributed to those in need.

food drive An organized community effort in which nonperishable foods are collected for distribution to the hungry.

food security Reliable access to sufficient and nutritious food to live a healthy life.

food stamp A U.S. government–issued stamp that can be exchanged for food.

humanitarian Charitable; concerning the improvement of people's lives.

hunger A weakened condition brought about by prolonged lack of food.

junk food Cheaply priced food that is high in calories but low in nutritional value.

malnourished Not getting an adequate amount of food in one's diet.

Parent-Teacher Associations (PTAs) Local organizations in which parents and teachers work together to benefit schools and students.

poverty The state of being poor.

poverty line A level of income below which a family is defined by the U.S. government to be living in poverty.

prevalence Regularity or usualness.

soup kitchen A place where food is contributed and distributed to the needy. (See also "food bank.")

starvation An extreme lack of food.

stigma A mark of disgrace or dishonor.

subsidized Partially funded by the U.S. government.

vouchers Coupons issued by the U.S. government that can be used to fund student's needs, whether it's getting fed or getting an education.

For More Information

Action Against Hunger-USA

247 West 37th Street, 10th Floor

New York, NY 10018

(212) 967-7800

Web site: http://www.actionagainsthunger.org
This international network attempts to save the lives
of hungry families. Its primary focus is on emergency
situations of conflict, natural disaster, and chronic food
insecurity.

America's Second Harvest

5 E. Wacker Drive, #2000

Chicago, IL 60601

(800) 771-2303

Web site: http://www.secondharvest.org
America's Second Harvest is the United States' largest
charitable hunger-relief organization.

Bread for the World Institute

50 F Street NW, Suite 500

Washington, DC 20001

(202) 639-9400

Web site: http://www.bread.org
This group works to educate the world about hunger in the
United States and abroad.

Congressional Hunger Center

Hall of the States Building

400 North Capitol Street NW, Suite G100

Washington, DC 20001

(202) 547-7022

Web site: http://www.hungercenter.org
This nonprofit group trains individuals to be leaders in the world fight against hunger.

Food Research and Action Center

1875 Connecticut Avenue NW, Suite 540

Washington, DC 20009

(202) 986-2200

Web site: http://www.frac.org
This national nonprofit organization works to eradicate hunger and malnutrition in the United States.

The Hunger Project-Canada

11 O'Connor Drive

Toronto, ON M4K 2K3

Canada

(416) 429-0023

Web site: http://www.thehungerproject.ca
This Canadian group raises awareness about chronic hunger in that country.

Oxfam Canada

250 City Centre Avenue, Suite 400

Ottawa, ON K1R 6K7

Canada

Web site: http://www.oxfam.ca

This Canadian chapter of Oxfam International fights hunger and other critical issues related to global poverty and injustice.

RESULTS/RESULTS Educational Fund

750 First Street NE, Suite 1040

Washington, DC 20002

(202) 783-2818

Web site: http://www.results.org

This nonprofit grassroots advocacy organization is committed to creating the political will to end hunger and poverty. The group tries to persuade elected officials to implement policy changes to combat hunger.

Web Sites

Due to the changing nature of Internet links, Rosen Publishing has developed an online list of Web sites related to the subject of this book. This site is updated regularly. Please use this link to access the list:

http://www.rosenlinks.com/itn/hung

For Further Reading

Fridell, Ron. *The War on Hunger: Dealing with Dictators, Deserts, and Debt*. Minneapolis, MN: Twenty-First Century Books, 2003.

Hunnicutt, Susan C. *World Hunger*. Detroit, MI: Greenhaven Press, 2006.

Jango-Cohen, Judith. *The History of Food*. Minneapolis, MN: Twenty-First Century Books, 2006.

Kamberg, Mary-Lane. *Bono: Fighting World Hunger and Poverty*. New York, NY: Rosen Publishing Group, 2008.

Kaye, Cathryn Berger. *A Kids' Guide to Hunger & Homelessness: How to Take Action!* Minneapolis, MN: Free Spirit Publishing, 2007.

Maddocks, Steven. *World Hunger*. Strongsville, OH: Gareth Stevens Publishing, 2004.

Mikkelsen, Jon. *Kids Against Hunger*. Mankato, MN: Stone Arch Books, 2009.

Bibliography

Feeding America. "Hunger and Poverty Statistics."
Retrieved August 23, 2008 (http://www.
feedingamerica.org/learn_about_hunger/fact_sheet/
poverty_stats.html?show_nce=1).

Garber, Kent. "The Growing Food Cost Crisis." *U.S. News
and World Report*, March 7, 2008. Retrieved
September 22, 2008 (www.usnews.com/articles/
news/2008/03/07/the-growing-food-cost-crisis.html).

National Public Radio. "Hunger in America."
November 2005. Retrieved August 10, 2008
(http://www.npr.org/templates/story/story.php?
storyId=5023829).

Nord, Mark, Margaret Andrews, and Steven Carlson.
"Household Food Security in the United States,
2006." Economic Research Report No. ERR-49,
November 2007.

Public Broadcasting System. "Hunger in America." April 11,
2008. Retrieved August 11, 2008 (www.pbs.org/
moyers/journal/04112008/profile4.html).

RESULTS. "U.S. Census: More Americans Below Poverty
Line in 2007 Than in 2001." August 26, 2008.
Retrieved September 20, 2008 (http://www.results.
org/website/article.asp?id=3626).

U.S. Department of Agriculture Economic Research Service. Various pages. Retrieved August 11– September 23, 2008 (http://www.ers.usda.gov).

U.S. Department of State. "2008 Poverty Guidelines." Retrieved August 28, 2008 (http://travel.state.gov/visa/immigrants/info/info_1327.html).

Weill, Jim. "The Impact of Rising Food Prices on Hunger in America." Presentation at the House Hunger Caucus Briefing, April 16, 2008. Retrieved August 11, 2008 (http://frac.org/pdf/JWhungercaucus_apr08.pdf).

Index

About the Author

Michael R. Wilson is a health and science writer. He has written on many topics for Rosen Publishing Group, including food additives, global health crises, the human brain, the cardiopulmonary system, and genetics.

Photo Credits

Cover (top left) © Chip Somodevilla/Getty Images (top right) © www.istockphoto.com/Timothy Goodwin; (bottom) © Mario Tama/Getty Images; pp. 4, 8 © www.istockphoto.com/Lynn Sneeden; p. 5 © Joe Raedie/Getty Images; pp. 6, 12, 17, 19, 27, 36, 42 © AP Photos; pp. 14, 16 © Chris Hondros/Getty Images; p. 21 © www.istockphoto.com/Peter Garbet; p. 24 © Don Emmert/ATF/Getty Images; pp. 28, 34 © Max Whittaker/Getty Images; p. 30 © Cindy Charles/Photo Edit; p. 32 © Kevin Fleming/Corbis; pp. 38, 40 ©Tim Boyle/Getty Images; pp. 45, 50 © David McNew/Getty Images; p. 47 ©Tim Boyle/Getty Images; p. 52 © Cynthia Jones/World Food Programme/Getty Images.

Designer: Tom Forget; Editor: Christopher Roberts
Photo Researcher: Marty Levick